Finditquick

INSECTS

A Golden Book • New York
Golden Books Publishing Company, Inc., New York, New York 10106

Created by Weigl Publishers Inc. for Golden Books Publishing Company, Inc.
Copyright © 2001 Golden Books Publishing Company, Inc.
All rights reserved. Printed in China.
No part of this book may be reproduced or copied in any form
without written permission from the copyright owner.
GOLDEN BOOKS®, A GOLDEN BOOK®, and FINDITQUICK™ are
trademarks of Golden Books Publishing Company, Inc.
Library of Congress Catalog Card Number: 00-106012
ISBN: 0-307-10532-6

How to Use This Book

The Internet is the coolest source of information available today. But finding what you're looking for isn't always easy. Have you ever spent hours searching for that hot new site only to end up lost in cyberspace?

This **finditquick** guide is designed to lead you to the best, most informative insect sites on the World Wide Web. In addition to getting the most up-to-date information, now you can watch breathtaking videos, see awesome photos, and hear voice clips, music, and sound effects.

In this guide you'll find:

Places To Go!
finditquick @

Take a virtual tour or visit a museum or event near you!

Things To Do!
finditquick @

Discover games, projects, and other online entertainment!

Brainteaser
Q
A

Shift your thinking into high gear with these puzzlers!

Insects Contents

Here's a list of thought-provoking questions you'll find inside. Each one will direct you to a site filled with answers, fun activities, and more links.

Which insect can live a week without a head? How do insects help police solve crimes? Which insect really tips the scales? Which bee is known for its bad attitude? Which insects help engineers create better jet planes? How do ants help the environment? Which insect is a worldwide killer? Which insects are like vampires? How can I protect myself from mosquito bites? Which insects build homes higher than 18 feet tall? Which bugs have been around since before the dinosaurs? Why do butterflies have dust on their wings? Where are insects considered a tasty treat? Which insects make homes out of paper? Which insects hope their mates will see the light? Which bugs are wanted by the FBID? Which insect can travel up to 2,000 miles? Which insect pulls a disappearing act? Which animals are related to insects? Which insects look like twigs and are often kept as pets? Which insects make their homes in people's scalps? When do ladybugs play "dead"? What do you call someone who studies insects? Why do bees make honey? What are the four stages in the life of a butterfly? Which insects was considered sacred in ancient Egypt? Which types of fabric do insects make? Are spiders a type of insect?

Which insect can live a week without a head?

finditquick @ http://www.yucky.com/roaches

Headless Wonders

A cockroach can live without its head. If you remove the cockroach's head, it will run around for about a week. The roach only dies of thirst because it doesn't have a mouth. With a head, a cockroach can survive without food for a month.

Vermin Vroom

Tropical cockroaches are the fastest moving insects on the ground. Their speed is equal to a person running at about 200 miles per hour! Adult male cockroaches can squeeze through spaces that are the thickness of a quarter.

Around the World

Cockroaches live all over the Earth. Most live in tropical regions, but some even exist at the North and South Poles. Cockroaches can survive in cold climates by living inside people's homes.

Brainteaser

Q: How many different types of cockroaches are there?

A: There are 5,000 species of cockroaches around the world.

How do insects help police solve crimes?

finditquick @ http://www.uio.no/ ~ mostarke/forens_ent/introduction.shtml

Inspector Insect

Forensic entomology is the use of insects to solve crimes. The presence of certain insects can tell police where a person or vehicle has been. Counting the type and number of insects present at a crime scene helps investigators figure out when and where a murder victim was killed.

Egg Evidence

By looking at insects, police can tell how long a victim has been dead. Insects such as blowflies lay their eggs on corpses within two days of the death. Because these insects hatch and mature in predictable stages, investigators can look at their development to estimate the victim's time of death.

At the Scene

Most of us are carrying around insects without even knowing it. By studying the types of insects found on shoes or car tires, forensic entomologists can guess where the criminal or vehicle has been based on the types of insects found.

Places To Go!

Explore the world of forensic entomology!

finditquick @

www.forensic-entomology.com

Which insect really tips the scales?

finditquick @ http://www.extremescience.com/BiggestBug.htm

Heavy Duty

The well-named Goliath beetle is a type of scarab beetle and the heaviest insect of all. Goliath beetles are about 4.5 inches long and weigh about 3.5 ounces. That's bigger than your hand!

Brainteaser

Q How dangerous is the sting of a killer bee?

A The sting is no more dangerous than that of other bees. They kill by attacking in swarms.

One Tough Customer

The Goliath beetle can survive in many different environments. Their hard outer shell, or exoskeleton, helps protect them from predators. Some beetles can trap moisture under their shell so that they won't dry out in desert areas. Other beetles can live underwater by breathing air that is trapped under their exoskeleton.

Giant Janitors

Goliath beetles and other waste-eating insects play an important role in keeping the environment healthy. By eating dead plants and dung, these beetles help keep Earth from being covered in animal and plant waste.

Which bee is known for its bad attitude?

finditquick @ http://agnews.tamu.edu/bees/

An Experiment Turned Bad

The killer bee is a cross between the gentle honeybee and the wild African bee. Brazilian beekeepers were trying to breed a better honeybee, but the result was not what they had hoped. The new bees are nasty and make less honey and beeswax.

Coming to a Town Near You

Killer bees were accidentally released to the wild in 1956. They have slowly been moving north from Brazil ever since.

Bee Attack!

Should you ever be unlucky enough to anger a swarm of killer bees, run fast in a straight line. Most people can outrun killer bees. Don't go underwater to try to get away from the bees. They'll just wait until you come up for air. If you are bitten, see a doctor.

Things To Do!

See the biggest, smallest, and fastest insects!

finditquick @ http://gnv.ifas.ufl.edu/~tjw/recbk.htm

Which insects help engineers create better jet planes?

finditquick @ http://www.wnet.org/nature/alienempire/hardware.html

Mystery Motion

Scientists don't know how insects fly! Scientists can use math to explain how airplanes and helicopters fly, but insect flight still can't be explained mathematically. Unlike the wings on an airplane, insect wings are constantly moving in different directions, which math can't calculate.

Building Fake Insects

Scientists make giant models of insects, like moths and dragonflies, and place them in wind tunnels to study how they fly. Smoke blown into the wind tunnel tells scientists how air moves around the insect's wings.

Mini Hovercrafts

Dragonflies are some of the best fliers in the insect world. They are speedy fliers, and can hover, stop, and change directions in an instant. Although engineers may never build jets that move as well as dragonflies, by studying insect flight they learn how to build better and faster planes.

Things To Do!

Grab your tweezers and go get some bugs!

finditquick @ http://www.uky.edu/Agriculture/Entomology/ythfacts/bugfun/collecti.htm

How do ants help the environment?

finditquick @ http://www.phoenixzoo.org/Pages/animals/leaf_cutter.html

Queen of the Hill

Each ant colony has a queen that lays all the eggs. Some very large colonies may have two or three queens. Drones, or male ants, mate with the queen to produce eggs. The drones die soon after mating.

Ant Gardeners

Leaf-cutter ants cut small pieces of plants and carry them back to their underground homes. The ants chew up the leaves and bury them in the soil to grow fungus. The chewed up leaves, fungus, and ant waste help to fertilize the soil.

Places To Go!

Find out more about insect wings and how they're used!

finditquick @

http://www.wf.carleton.ca/Museum/insects/insects.html

Guard Duty

Nurser ants are females that help care for the young. Worker ants are females that collect leaves and grow the fungus. Soldier ants, also females, are the largest ants, except for the queen. The soldiers help protect the colony.

Which insect is a worldwide killer?

finditquick @ http://www.insecta-inspecta.com/mosquitoes/malaria/index.html

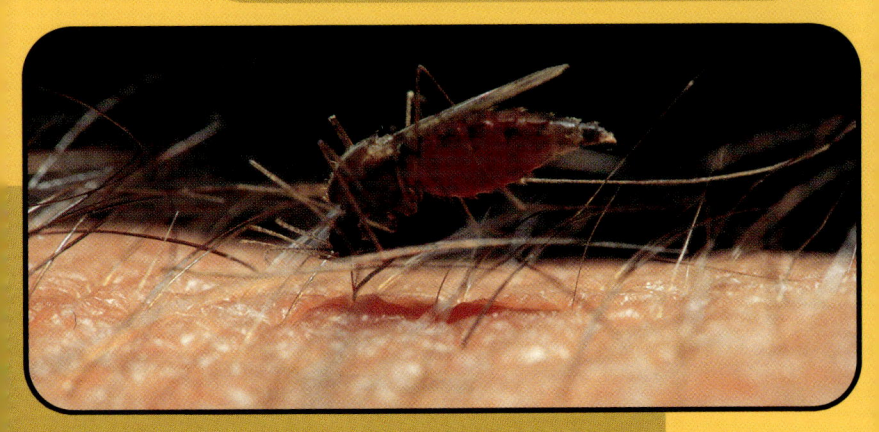

Bad Bites

The Anopheles mosquito causes malaria in people. Female mosquitoes transfer a deadly germ into the bloodstream when they bite. Male mosquitoes don't drink blood and therefore do not transmit malaria.

Incurable

Malaria attacks a person's liver. The symptoms of malaria include fever and vomiting. Malaria occurs in Mexico, most of South America and Africa, and parts of Asia. About 2 million people die from malaria each year around the world.

Deadly Diseases

As devastating as it is, malaria is only one of several diseases transmitted by mosquitoes. Dengue and yellow fever are two others. Together they affect more than 20 million people each year, and kill more than 50,000.

Brainteaser

Q Which disease killed 14 million people?

A The Bubonic Plague, which was spread by the Asian rat flea.

Which insects are like vampires?

finditquick @ http://www.ifas.ufl.edu/ ~ insect/livestock/bfly.htm

Bloodsuckers
Just like mosquitoes, adult female black flies drink the blood of people, livestock, and wild animals. Different species of black flies prefer the blood of different types of animals.

Aggressive Eaters
When a female black fly bites, she tears away a chunk of skin. The fly drinks the blood that pools in the wound. Black fly bites are especially painful because a hole is cut in the skin and can itch for several days. Like mosquitoes, black flies release anticoagulants into the bitten area. This prevents the wound from clotting and keeps fresh blood flowing for the insect to drink.

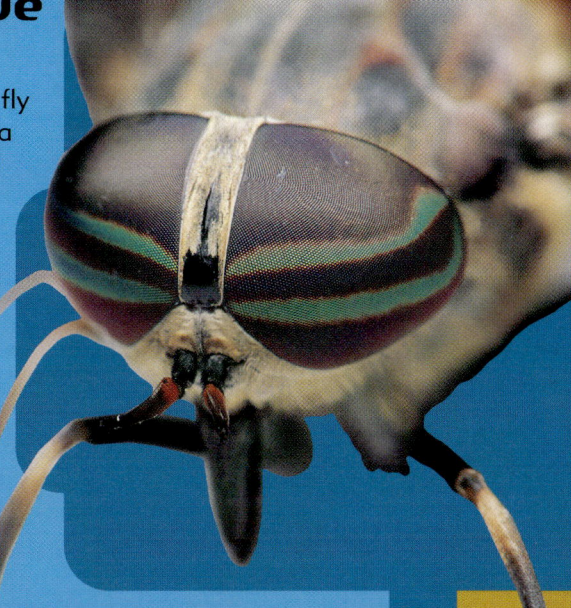

Places To Go!
Check out Antboy's Bugworld!

finditquick @
http://www.heatersworld.com/bugworld/

How can I protect myself from mosquito bites?

finditquick @ http://whyfiles.news.wisc.edu/016skeeter/self_protection.html

Timing Is Everything

It seems like mosquitoes are everywhere in the summertime, but if you know their habits, you can avoid them. Mosquitoes are the biggest problem in early summer, and they're most active at dawn and dusk. Mosquitoes stay away on windy days.

Things To Do!

Find out what's living on your pillow!

finditquick @ www.ehso.com/ehshome/DustMites.htm

A Batty Idea

One fun way to get rid of mosquitoes is to attract bats to the area. Bats can eat hundreds of mosquitoes an hour. Building a bat house will make your backyard more inviting.

Bug Off

Mosquito repellents, especially those that contain the chemical DEET, can help keep the mosquitoes away. There are also repellents that use natural ingredients like citronella. Bug zappers attract and kill mosquitoes, but they harm a lot of other bugs, too.

Which insects build homes higher than 18 feet tall?

finditquick @ http://www.naturalpartners.org/InsectZoo/OrkinZoo/insectSoc.html

African Architects

African mound termites build homes out of soil and their saliva. Over many years, a termite mound can grow to a height of 18 feet or more. Termite mounds have thick insulating walls to help keep the temperature constant inside the mound.

Crowded House

Large termite mounds may contain more than 2 million termites. Termite queens can live fifteen years and lay 6,000 to 7,000 eggs each day.

Crafty Critters

One type of termite in Australia is called the Compass Termite. Compass Termites always build their mounds with one long side running from north to south. This design allows the mound to soak up heat from the warm morning and afternoon sun.

Brainteaser

Q: What happens when termites listen to rock music?

A: Termites eat through wood twice as fast as normal when listening to rock music.

Which bugs have been around since before the dinosaurs?

finditquick @ http://powell.colgate.edu/wda/Beginners_Guide.htm

Older than T. rex

Fossils show that ancestors of the modern dragonfly lived over 300 million years ago. Why did the insects survive when the dinosaurs disappeared? Scientists have several theories as to why dragonfly-type insects are still around today.

Long Distance Travelers

In their adult stage, dragonflies travel far from where they spent their egg and larval stages. Even if the land in one area was no longer suitable for life, the dragonflies could travel almost anywhere else quickly and easily.

Deadly Design

Another survival theory has to do with the dragonfly's shape. Dragonflies have changed little over the years. Their body design makes them efficient at hunting in the air, meaning they have had little competition for their food supply.

Brainteaser

Q Exactly how strong are ants?

A Ants can lift up to 50 times their body weight.

Why do butterflies have dust on their wings?

finditquick @ http://www.mesc.usgs.gov/butterfly/butterfly-faq.html

Blossom Buddies

Bright colors and patterns of a butterfly's wings attract butterflies of the opposite sex for mating. We cannot see all of the patterns on some butterfly wings — some are only visible under ultraviolet light.

Colorful Camouflage

Many colorful butterflies are not very tasty. Some butterflies have bright colors, which warn potential predators that they will not make a good meal. Other butterflies have patterns that act as camouflage, allowing them to avoid predators by blending into their surroundings.

Things To Do!

Buy and release butterflies at your next party!

finditquick @ http://www.livebutterfly.com

Where are insects considered a tasty treat?

finditquick @ http://www.uky.edu/Agriculture/Entomology/ythfacts/bugfood/yf813.htm

A Delicious History

Many groups of people throughout history have eaten insects. People in Algeria cooked and ate locusts. The Aboriginal people of Australia have eaten many different types of insects, including witchetty grubs, which are said to taste like almonds.

Pass the Bugs, Please

People in Japan boil or fry up several types of insects to eat. Tokyo restaurants serve delicacies such as boiled wasp larvae and fried grasshoppers.

A Daily Dose of Bugs

Because it's impossible to keep insects out of food crops, much of the food you eat contains bugs or bug parts. Three-and-a-half ounces of chocolate may contain up to eighty tiny insect fragments!

Things To Do!

Try out some tasty insect recipes!

finditquick @ http://www.ent.iastate.edu/misc/insectsasfood.html

Which insects make homes out of paper?

finditquick @ http://fbox.vt.edu:10021/forestry/wildlife/stein/insects.html

I'll Huff, and I'll Puff...

Wasp nests look delicate, but they're actually quite sturdy. Wasps build their nests out of paper, which they make by chewing wood and mixing it with saliva.

Family Affair

A wasp nest is home to a whole family of wasps. A wasp community consists of one or more queens, male drones, and smaller female workers. The nests of most species of yellowjacket wasps have between 1,000 to 3,000 workers.

Home, Sweet Home

Not all wasps make their homes in paper nests. Some species dig burrows in the ground, others nest in hollow twigs, and some build nests completely of mud.

Brain Teaser

Q How are ants used to heal wounds?

A Ants bite through skin, their bodies are removed, and the heads are used as stitches.

Which insects hope their mates will see the light?

finditquick @ http://www.uky.edu/Agriculture/Entomology/ythfacts/allyr/yf807.htm

Light Trap

Some fungus gnats produce light in their larval stage. The larvae make a web on the walls of dark caves and use their light to attract other insects into the web. The larvae eat the insects trapped in their webs.

Morse Code

Fireflies can produce light in both their adult and larval stages. As adults, fireflies create light with organs inside their stomachs. They glow or flash their lights at night to attract mates. The larvae, called glowworms, shine their light on the ground.

Afterglow

A tiny, hopping insect called the springtail is another bug with a glowing history. Some springtails might glow constantly, with others glowing for just five or ten seconds. Scientists admit that they don't know much about how springtails produce light.

Things To Do!

Become an ant farmer!

finditquick @ http://www.uky.edu/Agriculture/Entomology/ythfacts/allyr/ants.htm

Which bugs are wanted by the FBID?

finditquick @ http://www.pbrc.hawaii.edu/ ~ kunkel/wanted/

Bad Things Come in Small Packages

Many insects can be annoying and somewhat harmful. There are even some insects that are deadly to people. Lice make their homes in people's scalps, causing itching and irritation. Tiny ticks attach themselves to the skin and suck blood. These bites can be irritating, but they can also spread dangerous illnesses such as Lyme Disease.

Stinging Insults

Ouch! Bee and wasp stings hurt, and they can be downright dangerous for some people with allergies. People who are allergic to the stings may swell up and have trouble breathing after being bitten. More than 2 million Americans are allergic to the stings of insects, such as bees and wasps.

Brainteaser

Q Which type of blood do mosquitoes like best?

A Mosquitoes would rather drink blood from cows than blood from people.

Which insect can travel up to 2,000 miles?

finditquick @ http://www.mbsf.org/facts.html

Tireless Travelers

The monarch butterfly is pretty particular about the weather. Spending warm days in Canada, these fair-weather friends head south at the first sign of winter. While some Monarchs fly to California, others will migrate to Mexico—2,000 miles away!

Staying In

Some monarch butterflies live in Hawaii and Florida. Naturally, they prefer the weather around home and leave the migration to their relatives up north.

A Passion for Poison

Monarch caterpillars' favorite meal is the toxic milkweed plant. This poison protects the insects from being eaten by lizards, frogs, birds and other animals. The monarch's bright, beautiful colors are a signal to other animals that they aren't good to eat.

Brainteaser

Q How do insects provide us with food?

A Insects pollinate plants that produce fruit and vegetables.

Which insect pulls a disappearing act?

finditquick @ http://www.animalsoftherainforest.com/prayingmantis.htm

Masters of Disguise

Praying mantises have the ability to blend into their environments. Most are green or brown and mix in with the branches or bark of the trees on which they live. The tropical flower mantis goes so far as to look like an actual flower.

Invisible Insect

Praying mantises will often sit still and wait for their prey to come to them. Since the mantises look so much like their surroundings, their prey don't see them until it's too late!

Things To Do!

Put your insect knowledge to the test and name the mystery bug!
finditquick @ http://www.uky.edu/Agriculture/Entomology/ythfacts/mystery/mystpic.htm

More than Meets the Eye

The praying mantis has many enemies. Birds and reptiles find this master of disguise to be a tasty treat. Fortunately for the praying mantis, it isn't always so easy to find.

Which animals are related to insects?

finditquick @ http://www.butterflies.org/teacherdownloads.htm

Meet the Arthropod Family

Insects are arthropods. Arthropods are animals that are cold-blooded, have jointed legs, and exoskeletons. Besides insects, there are four major types of arthropods: arachnids, crustaceans, millipedes, and centipedes.

Crusty Cousins

If you eat lobster or crab, you're practically eating bugs. Lobsters, crabs, shrimp, barnacles, and tiny water fleas are crustaceans—close cousins of insects. Most crustaceans live in saltwater, but some, like the wood louse, live on land.

Lotsa Legs

Centipedes and millipedes look like a cross between an insect and a worm, but they're actually types of arthropods. These creepy-crawlies don't really have hundreds of legs, but they do have one pair of legs for each segment of their bodies.

Places To Go!

Learn how to start your own butterfly garden!

finditquick @
http://www.butterflies.org

22

Which insects look like twigs and are often kept as pets?

finditquick @ http://www.ex.ac.uk/bugclub/sticks.html

Sticking Around

Stick insects are long, thin bugs that resemble leaves, twigs or flowers. Most stick insects live in hot, humid climates, but they can be kept indoors as pets. With the right conditions, stick insects can be quite happy living in cages.

Red Light Zone

Use a light bulb to keep your stick insect's cage cozy. Make sure the bulb is out of reach, so your pet can't burn itself. Sticklers for detail, stick insects prefer gentle red lights at night.

Sticking It to You

Some species of stick insect will bite or pinch if handled roughly. Others release a defensive chemical spray, which can cause pain or even temporary blindness.

Things To Do!

Test your knowledge about insects with quiz cards!

finditquick @ http://entowww.tamu.edu/academic/ucourses/ento489/material/cardgame1.html

Which insects make their homes in people's scalps?

finditquick @ http://www.headlice.org/faq/lousology.html

How to Get a Head in Life

Itchy scalp? Check your head for lice! Head lice are tiny wingless insects that feed on human blood. They are about the size of sesame seeds and can live up to thirty days.

Nit Picking

A female louse can lay up to 100 eggs, called nits. The nits are attached to hair at the scalp. They take about a week to hatch and another week to start laying their own nits.

Good Grooming

Head lice can be difficult to get rid of because they are so small, and they lay so many eggs. Special shampoos can help kill the adult lice, while combing with fine-toothed combs can get rid of the nits.

Things To Do!

Print out some Bug-go cards and play this insect bingo game!

finditquick @ http://www.uky.edu/Agriculture/IPM/teachers/bug-go/bug-go.htm